In My Backyard

I SEE A BIRD

By Alex Appleby

Gareth Stevens Publishing

Please visit our website, www.garethstevens.com. For a free color catalog of all our high-quality books, call toll free 1-800-542-2595 or fax 1-877-542-2596.

Library of Congress Cataloging-in-Publication Data

Appleby, Alex.
I see a bird / Alex Appleby.
p. cm. — (In my backyard)
Includes index.
ISBN 978-1-4339-8540-9 (pbk.)
ISBN 978-1-4339-8541-6 (6-pack)
ISBN 978-1-4339-8539-3 (library binding)
1. Birds—Juvenile literature. I. Title.
QL676.2.A66 2013
598—dc23
2012022023

First Edition

Published in 2013 by
Gareth Stevens Publishing
111 East 14th Street, Suite 349
New York, NY 10003

Editor: Ryan Nagelhout
Designer: Katelyn Londino

Photo credits: Cover, pp. 1, 9, 15, 17, 23, 24 (nest, feathers) iStockphoto/Thinkstock.com; p. 5 Simon_g/Shutterstock.com; p. 7 Victor Tyakht/Shutterstock.com; pp. 11, 24 (bill) zakharov aleksey/Shutterstock.com; p. 13 © iStockphoto.com/SoopySue; p. 19 D&D Photos/Shutterstock.com; p. 21 Stockbyte/Thinkstock.com.

Printed in the United States of America

CPSIA compliance information: Batch #CW13GS: For further information contact Gareth Stevens, New York, New York at 1-800-542-2595.

Contents

Taking Flight 4

Home Sweet Home 8

Types of Birds 12

Words to Know 24

Index. 24

A bird can fly!

It has big arms
that help it fly.
These are called wings.

It builds a nest in a tree.
This is its home.

It has a very hard mouth.
This is called its bill.

There are many kinds of birds.

Bluebirds love to sing!

Cardinals have
bright red feathers.

A robin's eggs are bright blue.

An oriole's nest hangs below tree branches.

A blue jay can change its birdcall. It often sounds like a hawk!

Words to Know

bill

feathers

nest

Index

bill 10

feathers 16

nest 8, 20

wings 6